FOL

A GUIDE TO ARIZONA'S INDEPENDENT CRAFT BREWERIES

by Paige Warren and Jef Johann

ArizonaBrewTrek.com
info@ArizonaBrewTrek.com

Arizona Brew Trek
Follow the Beer

Copyright © 2018 Arizona Brew Trek, LLC

**Various brewery information provided by
company websites and social media, therefore
may not reflect the most accurate features.
Check the brewery's website, or call before
visiting.**

Cover Design and Artwork: Thomas Barton
Interior Design and Formatting: Deborah J Ledford

Print Format ISBN: 978-1724629760

Welcome to Arizona Brew Trek, a unique opportunity to experience all of Arizona's locally owned and operated, independent craft breweries, while exploring the beautiful state of Arizona. We want to encourage in-state travel for people who might be new to Arizona, tourists, or residents of Arizona who are ready to go on an adventure. Whether you are making your way to the Grand Canyon, hiking up to Arizona's highest peak, Mt. Humphrey's, or visiting the historic mining town of Bisbee, you are sure to pass a few breweries along the way! *Follow the Beer* is your personal guide book and passport to all breweries around Arizona.

Enjoy the journey!

HOW TO USE THIS GUIDE

First and foremost: Have Fun and Be Safe! Always have a Designated Driver! Bring your growler to fill and enjoy the beer after you are finished driving for the day!

Use this book to help you plan your next adventure! Visit somewhere in Arizona you have never been, try something new and make new memories! Whether you are traveling across the city or state, you can easily map out the breweries in the general area you plan to visit.

We divided the breweries into regions: Northern, Central and Southern Arizona. We also have a complete list of breweries in alphabetical order to easily find the brewery you are looking for. The AZBT Map will give you a general idea of where each city is located within the region and State. Please note that we did not include every listed city within Phoenix Metropolitan area due to limited space.

In each brewery listing, we have included general information on each brewery. The Legend will help you quickly find out what each brewery offers to their patrons.

For directions to each location, you can locate the brewery listing on www.arizonabrewtrek.com which will take you to the brewery's Google listing, or simply ask Google for directions.

Before you embark on your Brew Trek, please contact breweries for their hours of operation! Many breweries here in Arizona, especially the smaller ones, have limited hours of operation. Plan ahead!

HOW TO USE THIS GUIDE

At the brewery, ask them to stamp your passport! Each brewery page has space for an individual stamp. Please be patient and respectful if the brewery is busy and or unable to stamp your book. Get creative! Ask for, or purchase, a sticker!

Last, don't forget to jot down the beers your tried, what you liked the most and any notes you want to make for yourself. Remember, you are making memories here! Then look for your favorite craft beers when you are at restaurants, markets or places where they locally sell Arizona Craft Beer!

We are on social media and would love to follow your favorite adventures! Tag yourself and friends @AZBrewtrek with #AZBT on Instagram, Facebook and Twitter.

Icon Legend:

🍴 = Food Available

🎸 = Live Music

🐾 = Dog Friendly

🚲 = Bicycle Parking

🏍 = Motorcycle Parking

🎯 = Darts and/or Games

🚚 = Food Truck

This copy of *Follow the Beer* belongs to:

_____

Date your journey began:

_____

PLEASE DRINK RESPONSIBLY

Always plan ahead and have a
designated driver or use Rideshare!

Arizona Brew Trek has partnered with
Lyft to offer Brew Trek Riders
20% off 10 Rides
when you enter the code:
AZBREWTREK

BREWERIES LIST

BREWERIES (cont)

BREWERIES (cont)

BREWERIES (cont)

COMING SOON
[Check Brewery Websites for Updates]

Castle Hot Springs Brewery - Morristown
Pedal Haus Brewery - Phoenix
Sentinel Peak Brewing - Downtown Tucson
State 48 Lager House - Scottsdale
Uncle Bear's Brewery - Gilbert

Click or scan the QR Code for full list of breweries
at the Arizona Brew Trek website

AZBT MAP

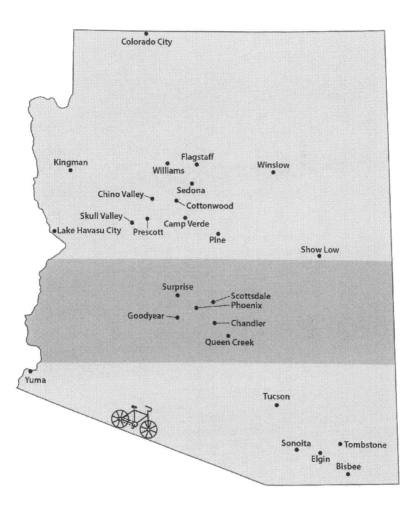

BEER STYLES

PALE LAGER

Soft Malt Taste • Light Body • Dry Finish • Best If New
To Craft Beers • Bitterness 20-40 Units

BLONDE ALE

Mild Malt Sweetness • Low Bitterness • Light Body
• Dry Finish • Great For Beginners
Bitterness 20-30 Units

PALE ALE / INDIAN PALE ALE

Strikes Balance Between Malt And Hops • Medium To
Dry Finish • Much Higher Bitterness
Bitterness 50-100 Units

AMBER ALE

Well-Balanced Hops & Malts • Caramel Richness
Medium Body • Bitterness 20-60 Units

RED ALE

Toasted Malt • Medium Sweet Caramel Flavour
• Dry Finish • Bitterness 50-100 Units

BROWN ALE

Mild To High Malt Character • Low Hops
• Caramel • Chocolate • Toffee • Nuts
• Biscuit Flavours • Medium Dry Finish
Bitterness 20-60 Units

PORTER

Roasted Malt Taste With Notes Of Chocolate
• Medium Dry Finish • Dark Color • Little Fizz
• Not Recommend For Beginners
Bitterness 30-60 Units

STOUT

Strong Roasted Malt Taste & Coffee
• Chocolate Caramel Flavors • Dark Color • Little Fizz
• Not Recommend For Beginners
Bitterness 30-60 Units

CENTRAL ARIZONA

ALPHABETICAL LISTING - Central Arizona Breweries

12 West Brewing
8-Bit Aleworks
Arizona Wilderness Brewing Co
Barrio Brewing Co - Mesa
Beer Research Institute
Blasted Barley Beer Co
Bone Haus Brewing
Cave Creek Beer Co
Craft 64
Deep Roots Brewing
Desert Eagle Brewing Company - Falcon Field
Desert Eagle Brewing Company - Mesa
Desert Monks Brewing Co
Dubina Brewing
Flying Basset Brewing
Freak'N Brewing Company
Goldwater Brewing Co
Grand Avenue Brewing Company
Helio Basin Brewing Company
HELLUVA Brewing Company
Helton Brewing Company
H.O.P. Central Brewing Co and Taproom
Huss Brewing Co Taproom - Uptown Plaza
Huss Brewing Company - Tempe
Lochiel Brewing
Loco Patron - Mexican Brewery & Kitchen
McFate Brewing Company - North Scottsdale
McFate Brewing Company - South Scottsdale
Mesquite River Brewing
Mother Bunch Brewing
North Mountain Brewing Co
O.H.S.O. Brewery - Gilbert
O.H.S.O. - North Scottsdale
O.H.S.O. - Paradise Valley
O.H.S.O. Eatery & Nano-Brewery - Arcadia

ALPHABETICAL LISTING - Central Arizona Breweries

Old Ellsworth Brewing Co
Oro Brewing Company
Pedal Haus Brewery - Tempe
Peoria Artisan Brewery
Perch Pub Brewery
Richter Aleworks
Saddle Mountain Brewing Company
SanTan Brewing Company - Chandler
SanTan Brewing Company - Phoenix
Scottsdale Beer Company
Sleepy Dog Saloon & Brewery
Sonoran Brewing Company
State 48 Funk House Brewery
State 48 Brewery DTPHX
State 48 Brewery - Surprise
SunUp Brewing Company
The Phoenix Ale Brewery
The Phoenix Ale Brewery Central Kitchen
The Shop Beer Co
Transplant City Beer Company
Two Brothers Tap House and Brewery
Uncle Bear's Brewery - Phoenix
Uncle Bear's Grill & Tap - Mesa
Uncle Bear's Grill & Tap - Queen Creek
Walter Station Brewery
Wren House Brewing Company

12 West Brewing

3000 E Ray Rd, Barnone Bldg 6, Ste 110, Gilbert, 85296
480-404-9699

Date Visited: _____

Rating: 🍺 🍺 🍺 🍺 🍺   stamp

BEERS TRIED:

_____

_____

_____

ADDITIONAL SPECIAL FEATURES:

Outdoor Seating
Outside Food Allowed

Favorite Brew – Likes – Dislikes – Notes:

_____

_____

_____

_____

_____

Visited With: _____

Best Time of Year to Visit: _____Visit Again: Y / N

8-Bit Aleworks

1050a North Fairway Dr, #101, Avondale, 85323
623-925-1650

Date Visited: _____

Rating: 🍺 🍺 🍺 🍺 🍺

stamp

BEERS TRIED:

_____

_____

_____

ADDITIONAL SPECIAL FEATURES:

Nostalgic 8-Bit Theme

Favorite Brew – Likes – Dislikes – Notes:

_____

_____

_____

_____

_____

Visited With: _____

Best Time of Year to Visit: _____Visit Again: Y / N

Arizona Wilderness Brewing Co

721 N Arizona Ave, #103, Gilbert, 85233
480-497-2739

Date Visited: _____

Rating: 🍺 🍺 🍺 🍺 🍺

stamp

BEERS TRIED:

_____

_____

_____

🍴 🐾 🎸 🚲 🏍

ADDITIONAL SPECIAL FEATURES:

Happy Hour

Outdoor Patio

Kid Friendly

Favorite Brew – Likes – Dislikes – Notes:

_____

_____

_____

_____

_____

Visited With: _____

Best Time of Year to Visit: _____Visit Again: Y / N

Barrio Brewing Co –

Mesa Location
5803 S Sossaman Rd, Mesa, 85212
480-988-7171

Date Visited: _____

Rating: 🍺 🍺 🍺 🍺 🍺

stamp

BEERS TRIED:

_____

_____

_____

🍴

ADDITIONAL SPECIAL FEATURES:

Happy Hour
Located in Phoenix-Mesa Gateway Airport

Favorite Brew – Likes – Dislikes – Notes:

_____

_____

_____

_____

_____

Visited With: _____

Best Time of Year to Visit: _____Visit Again: Y / N

Beer Research Institute

1641 S Stapley Dr, Mesa, 85204
480-892-2020

Date Visited: _____

Rating: 🍺 🍺 🍺 🍺 🍺

stamp

BEERS TRIED:

_____

_____

_____

🍴 🐾 ⚙ 🚲 🏍

ADDITIONAL SPECIAL FEATURES:

Happy Hour
Outdoor Patio   Kid Friendly

Favorite Brew – Likes – Dislikes – Notes:

_____

_____

_____

_____

_____

Visited With: _____

Best Time of Year to Visit: _____Visit Again: Y / N

Blasted Barley Beer Co

404 S Mill Ave, Tempe, 85281
480-967-5887

Date Visited: _____

Rating: 🍺 🍺 🍺 🍺 🍺

stamp

BEERS TRIED:

_____

_____

_____

🍴 ❀

ADDITIONAL SPECIAL FEATURES:

Happy Hour

Outdoor Seating   Kid Friendly

Favorite Brew – Likes – Dislikes – Notes:

_____

_____

_____

_____

_____

Visited With: _____

Best Time of Year to Visit: _____Visit Again: Y / N

Bone Haus Brewing

15825 E Shea Blvd, Suite 101, Fountain Hills, 85268
480-980-3579

Date Visited: _____

Rating: 🍺 🍺 🍺 🍺 🍺   stamp

BEERS TRIED:

_____

_____

_____

ADDITIONAL SPECIAL FEATURES:

_____

Favorite Brew – Likes – Dislikes – Notes:

_____

_____

_____

_____

_____

Visited With: _____

Best Time of Year to Visit: _____Visit Again: Y / N

Cave Creek Beer Co

7100 E Cave Creek Rd, Cave Creek, 85331
480-488-2187

Date Visited: _____

Rating: 🍺 🍺 🍺 🍺 🍺

stamp

BEERS TRIED:

_____

_____

_____

🍴 🏍️

ADDITIONAL SPECIAL FEATURES:

Happy Hour

Outdoor Seating   Kid Friendly

Favorite Brew – Likes – Dislikes – Notes:

_____

_____

_____

_____

_____

Visited With: _____

Best Time of Year to Visit: _____Visit Again: Y / N

Craft 64

6922 East Main St, Scottsdale, 85251
480-946-0542

Date Visited: _____

Rating: 🍺 🍺 🍺 🍺 🍺   stamp

BEERS TRIED:

_____

_____

_____

🍴 🐾 🚲

ADDITIONAL SPECIAL FEATURES:

Outdoor Seating

Favorite Brew – Likes – Dislikes – Notes:

_____

_____

_____

_____

_____

Visited With: _____

Best Time of Year to Visit: _____ Visit Again: Y / N

Deep Roots Brewing

821 N 2nd St, Phoenix, 85004
602-330-6790

Date Visited: _____

Rating: 🍺 🍺 🍺 🍺 🍺

stamp

BEERS TRIED:

_____

_____

_____

ADDITIONAL SPECIAL FEATURES:

Package & Retail Beer, Wine and Liquor to Go

Favorite Brew – Likes – Dislikes – Notes:

_____

_____

_____

_____

_____

Visited With: _____

Best Time of Year to Visit: _____Visit Again: Y / N

Desert Eagle Brewing Company –
Falcon Field
2613 N Thunderbird Cir, Mesa, 85215
480-699-8781

Date Visited: _____

Rating: 🍺 🍺 🍺 🍺 🍺

stamp

BEERS TRIED:

_____

_____

_____

🍴 🎸 🏍️

ADDITIONAL SPECIAL FEATURES:

_____

Favorite Brew – Likes – Dislikes – Notes:

_____

_____

_____

_____

_____

Visited With: _____

Best Time of Year to Visit: _____Visit Again: Y / N

Desert Eagle Brewing Company
Mesa Location
150 W Main St, Mesa, 85201
480-656-2662

Date Visited: _____

Rating: 🍺 🍺 🍺 🍺 🍺   stamp

BEERS TRIED:

_____

_____

_____

🍴 🎸 🏍️

ADDITIONAL SPECIAL FEATURES:

_____

Favorite Brew – Likes – Dislikes – Notes:

_____

_____

_____

_____

_____

Visited With: _____

Best Time of Year to Visit: _____Visit Again: Y / N

Desert Monks Brewing Co

1094 S Gilbert Rd, #101, Gilbert, 85296
480-525-7444

Date Visited: _____

Rating: 🍺 🍺 🍺 🍺 🍺

stamp

BEERS TRIED:

_____

_____

_____

ADDITIONAL SPECIAL FEATURES:

_____

Favorite Brew – Likes – Dislikes – Notes:

_____

_____

_____

_____

_____

Visited With: _____

Best Time of Year to Visit: _____Visit Again: Y / N

Dubina Brewing

17035 N 67th Ave, #6, Glendale, 85308
623-412-7770

Date Visited: _____

Rating: 🍺 🍺 🍺 🍺 🍺

stamp

BEERS TRIED:

_____

_____

_____

🍴 🏍 ⚙

ADDITIONAL SPECIAL FEATURES:

Kid Friendly

Favorite Brew – Likes – Dislikes – Notes:

_____

_____

_____

_____

_____

Visited With: _____

Best Time of Year to Visit: _____Visit Again: Y / N

Flying Basset Brewing

720 W Ray Rd, Gilbert, 85233
480-426-1373

Date Visited: _____

Rating: 🍺 🍺 🍺 🍺 🍺   stamp

BEERS TRIED:

_____

_____

_____

🍴 🐾 🚲 ❀

ADDITIONAL SPECIAL FEATURES:

Happy Hour

Outdoor Seating   Good for Groups

Favorite Brew – Likes – Dislikes – Notes:

_____

_____

_____

_____

_____

Visited With: _____

Best Time of Year to Visit: _____Visit Again: Y / N

Freak'N Brewing Company

9299 W Olive Ave, #513, Peoria, 85345
623-738-5804

Date Visited: _____

Rating: 🍺 🍺 🍺 🍺 🍺

stamp

BEERS TRIED:

_____

_____

_____

🏍 ✹

ADDITIONAL SPECIAL FEATURES:

Happy Hour

Favorite Brew – Likes – Dislikes – Notes:

_____

_____

_____

_____

_____

Visited With: _____

Best Time of Year to Visit: _____Visit Again: Y / N

Goldwater Brewing Co

3608 N Scottsdale Rd, Scottsdale, 85251
480-350-7305

Date Visited: _____

Rating: 🍺 🍺 🍺 🍺 🍺   stamp

BEERS TRIED:

_____

_____

_____

🐾 🚲 ❀

ADDITIONAL SPECIAL FEATURES:

Outdoor Seating   Kid Friendly
Underground Taproom   Upstairs Patio

Favorite Brew – Likes – Dislikes – Notes:

_____

_____

_____

_____

_____

Visited With: _____

Best Time of Year to Visit: _____Visit Again: Y / N

Grand Avenue Brewing Company

1205 W Pierce St, Phoenix, 85007
602-670-5465

Date Visited: _____

Rating: 🍺 🍺 🍺 🍺 🍺

BEERS TRIED:

_____

_____

_____

🍴 🚲 🏍️

ADDITIONAL SPECIAL FEATURES:

_____

Favorite Brew – Likes – Dislikes – Notes:

_____

_____

_____

_____

_____

Visited With: _____

Best Time of Year to Visit: _____Visit Again: Y / N

Helio Basin Brewing Company

3935 E Thomas Rd, Phoenix, 85018
602-354-3525

Date Visited: _____

Rating: 🍺 🍺 🍺 🍺 🍺

stamp

BEERS TRIED:

_____

_____

_____

🍴 🍺 🚲 ❀

ADDITIONAL SPECIAL FEATURES:

Happy Hour

Favorite Brew – Likes – Dislikes – Notes:

_____

_____

_____

_____

_____

Visited With: _____

Best Time of Year to Visit: _____Visit Again: Y / N

HELLUVA Brewing Company

3950 W Ray Rd, Chandler, 85226
480-664-0220

Date Visited: _____

Rating: 🍺 🍺 🍺 🍺 🍺

stamp

BEERS TRIED:

_____

_____

_____

ADDITIONAL SPECIAL FEATURES:

Happy Hour

Outdoor Seating   Kid Friendly

Favorite Brew – Likes – Dislikes – Notes:

_____

_____

_____

_____

_____

Visited With: _____

Best Time of Year to Visit: _____Visit Again: Y / N

Helton Brewing Company

2144 E Indian School Rd, Phoenix, 85016
602-730-2739

Date Visited: _____

Rating: 🍺 🍺 🍺 🍺 🍺   stamp

BEERS TRIED:

_____

_____

_____

🍴 🎸 🚲 ☸

ADDITIONAL SPECIAL FEATURES:

Outdoor Beer Garage

Favorite Brew – Likes – Dislikes – Notes:

_____

_____

_____

_____

_____

Visited With: _____

Best Time of Year to Visit: _____Visit Again: Y / N

H.O.P. Central Brewing Co and Taproom

5505 W Ray Rd, Suite 2, Chandler, 85226
480-284-6320

Date Visited: _____

Rating: 🍺 🍺 🍺 🍺 🍺

stamp

BEERS TRIED:

_____

_____

_____

ADDITIONAL SPECIAL FEATURES:

Happy Hour
Outside Food Allowed

Favorite Brew – Likes – Dislikes – Notes:

_____

_____

_____

_____

_____

Visited With: _____

Best Time of Year to Visit: _____Visit Again: Y / N

Huss Brewing Co Taproom –

Uptown Plaza, Phoenix
100 E Camelback Rd, #160, Phoenix, 85012
602-441-4677

Date Visited: _____

Rating: 🍺 🍺 🍺 🍺 🍺   stamp

BEERS TRIED:

_____

_____

_____

🍴 🐾 🚲 🏍 ☸

ADDITIONAL SPECIAL FEATURES:

Happy Hour
Kid Friendly

Favorite Brew – Likes – Dislikes – Notes:

_____

_____

_____

_____

_____

Visited With: _____

Best Time of Year to Visit: _____Visit Again: Y / N

Huss Brewing Company –

Tempe Location
1520 W Mineral Rd, Suite 102, Tempe, 85283
480-264-7611

Date Visited: _____

Rating: 🍺 🍺 🍺 🍺 🍺   stamp

BEERS TRIED:

_____

_____

_____

ADDITIONAL SPECIAL FEATURES:

Happy Hour
Outside Food Allowed

Favorite Brew – Likes – Dislikes – Notes:

_____

_____

_____

_____

_____

Visited With: _____

Best Time of Year to Visit: _____Visit Again: Y / N

Lochiel Brewing

7143 E Southern Ave, #131, Mesa, 85209
480-666-0915

Date Visited: _____

Rating: 🍺 🍺 🍺 🍺 🍺   stamp

BEERS TRIED:

_____

_____

_____

❊

ADDITIONAL SPECIAL FEATURES:

Outside Food Allowed

Favorite Brew – Likes – Dislikes – Notes:

_____

_____

_____

_____

_____

Visited With: _____

Best Time of Year to Visit: _____Visit Again: Y / N

Loco Patron

Mexican Brewery & Kitchen

14950 N Northsight Blvd, Scottsdale, 85260
480-699-7271

Date Visited: _____

Rating: 🍺 🍺 🍺 🍺 🍺

stamp

BEERS TRIED:

_____

_____

_____

🍴 🎸 🐾 🚲 🏍 ☸

ADDITIONAL SPECIAL FEATURES:

Happy Hour
Outdoor Seating

Favorite Brew – Likes – Dislikes – Notes:

_____

_____

_____

_____

_____

Visited With: _____

Best Time of Year to Visit: _____Visit Again: Y / N

McFate Brewing Company –

North Scottsdale

7337 E Shea Blvd, Suite 105, Scottsdale, 85260
480-994-1275

Date Visited: _____

Rating: 🍺 🍺 🍺 🍺 🍺   stamp

BEERS TRIED:

_____

_____

_____

🍴 🐾 🚲 🏍️

ADDITIONAL SPECIAL FEATURES:

Happy Hour

Sunday Brunch

Outdoor Seating   Kid Friendly

Favorite Brew – Likes – Dislikes – Notes:

_____

_____

_____

_____

_____

Visited With: _____

Best Time of Year to Visit: _____ Visit Again: Y / N

McFate Brewing Company –
South Scottsdale
1312 N Scottsdale Rd, Scottsdale, 85257
480-656-9100

Date Visited: _____

Rating: 🍺 🍺 🍺 🍺 🍺   stamp

BEERS TRIED:

_____

_____

_____

🍴 🐾 🚲 🏍

ADDITIONAL SPECIAL FEATURES:

Happy Hour   Sunday Brunch
Outdoor Seating   Kid Friendly

Favorite Brew – Likes – Dislikes – Notes:

_____

_____

_____

_____

_____

Visited With: _____

Best Time of Year to Visit: _____Visit Again: Y / N

Mesquite River Brewing aka MRB

13610 N Scottsdale Rd, #18, Scottsdale, 85254
480-656-7696

Date Visited: _____

Rating: 🍺 🍺 🍺 🍺 🍺   stamp

BEERS TRIED:

_____

_____

_____

🍴 🎸 🏍 ⚙

ADDITIONAL SPECIAL FEATURES:

Outside Food Allowed   Kid Friendly

Favorite Brew – Likes – Dislikes – Notes:

_____

_____

_____

_____

_____

Visited With: _____

Best Time of Year to Visit: _____Visit Again: Y / N

Mother Bunch Brewing

825 N 7th St, Phoenix, 85006
602-368-3580

Date Visited: _____

Rating: 🍺 🍺 🍺 🍺 🍺

stamp

BEERS TRIED:

_____

_____

_____

🍴 🎸 🚲 🎯

ADDITIONAL SPECIAL FEATURES:

Happy Hour
Kid Friendly

Favorite Brew – Likes – Dislikes – Notes:

_____

_____

_____

_____

_____

Visited With: _____

Best Time of Year to Visit: _____Visit Again: Y / N

North Mountain Brewing Co

522 E Dunlap Ave, Phoenix, 85020
602-861-5999

Date Visited: _____

Rating: 🍺 🍺 🍺 🍺 🍺   stamp

BEERS TRIED:

_____

_____

_____

🍴 🎸 🐾 🚲 ✹

ADDITIONAL SPECIAL FEATURES:

Happy Hour
Outdoor Seating   Kid Friendly

Favorite Brew – Likes – Dislikes – Notes:

_____

_____

_____

_____

_____

Visited With: _____

Best Time of Year to Visit: _____Visit Again: Y / N

O.H.S.O. – Gilbert

355 N Gilbert Rd, Suite 102, Gilbert, 85234
602-900-9004

Date Visited: _____

Rating: 🍺 🍺 🍺 🍺 🍺   stamp

BEERS TRIED:

_____

_____

_____

🍴 🐾 🚲 🏍 ⚙

ADDITIONAL SPECIAL FEATURES:

Happy Hour

Outdoor Seating   Kid Friendly

Favorite Brew – Likes – Dislikes – Notes:

_____

_____

_____

_____

_____

Visited With: _____

Best Time of Year to Visit: _____Visit Again: Y / N

O.H.S.O. – North Scottsdale

15681 N Hayden Rd, #112, Scottsdale, 85260
480-948-3159

Date Visited: _____

Rating: 🍺 🍺 🍺 🍺 🍺

stamp

BEERS TRIED:

_____

_____

_____

🍴 🐾 🚲 🏍 ⚙

ADDITIONAL SPECIAL FEATURES:

Happy Hour

Outdoor Seating   Kid Friendly

Favorite Brew – Likes – Dislikes – Notes:

_____

_____

_____

_____

_____

Visited With: _____

Best Time of Year to Visit: _____Visit Again: Y / N

O.H.S.O. – Paradise Valley

10810 N Tatum Blvd, #126, Phoenix, 85028
602-900-9003

Date Visited: _____

Rating: 🍺 🍺 🍺 🍺 🍺   stamp

BEERS TRIED:

_____

_____

_____

🍴 🐾 🚲 🏍 ☸

ADDITIONAL SPECIAL FEATURES:

Happy Hour

Outdoor Seating   Kid Friendly

Favorite Brew – Likes – Dislikes – Notes:

_____

_____

_____

_____

_____

Visited With: _____

Best Time of Year to Visit: _____Visit Again: Y / N

O.H.S.O. Eatery & Nano–Brewery
Arcadia

4900 E Indian School Rd, Phoenix, 85018
602-955-0358

Date Visited: _____

Rating: 🍺 🍺 🍺 🍺 🍺

stamp

BEERS TRIED:

_____

_____

_____

🍴 🐾 🚲 🏍 ☸

ADDITIONAL SPECIAL FEATURES:

Happy Hour

Outdoor Seating   Kid Friendly

Favorite Brew – Likes – Dislikes – Notes:

_____

_____

_____

_____

_____

Visited With: _____

Best Time of Year to Visit: _____ Visit Again: Y / N

Old Ellsworth Brewing Co

22005 S Ellsworth Rd, Queen Creek, 85142
480-935-2796

Date Visited: _____

Rating: 🍺 🍺 🍺 🍺 🍺

stamp

BEERS TRIED:

_____

_____

_____

🍴 🐾 🚲 🏍️

ADDITIONAL SPECIAL FEATURES:

Happy Hour

Outdoor Seating   Kid Friendly

Favorite Brew – Likes – Dislikes – Notes:

_____

_____

_____

_____

_____

Visited With: _____

Best Time of Year to Visit: _____Visit Again: Y / N

Oro Brewing Company
210 W Main St, Mesa, 85201
480-398-8247

Date Visited: _____

Rating: 🍺 🍺 🍺 🍺 🍺   stamp

BEERS TRIED:

_____

_____

_____

🍴 🐾 🚲 ☸

ADDITIONAL SPECIAL FEATURES:

Happy Hour
Outdoor Seating

Favorite Brew – Likes – Dislikes – Notes:

_____

_____

_____

_____

_____

Visited With: _____

Best Time of Year to Visit: _____Visit Again: Y / N

Pedal Haus Brewery

730 S Mill Ave, #102, Tempe, 85281
480-314-2337

Date Visited: _____

Rating: 🍺 🍺 🍺 🍺 🍺

stamp

BEERS TRIED:

_____

_____

_____

🍴 🚲 ☸

ADDITIONAL SPECIAL FEATURES:

Happy Hour
Outdoor Seating

Favorite Brew – Likes – Dislikes – Notes:

_____

_____

_____

_____

_____

Visited With: _____

Best Time of Year to Visit: _____Visit Again: Y / N

Peoria Artisan Brewery

10144 N Lake Pleasant Pkwy, #1130, Peoria, 85382
623-572-2816

Date Visited: _____

Rating: 🍺 🍺 🍺 🍺 🍺   stamp

BEERS TRIED:

_____

_____

_____

🍴 🐾 🚲 🏍️

ADDITIONAL SPECIAL FEATURES:

Happy Hour

Outdoor Seating   Kid Friendly

Favorite Brew – Likes – Dislikes – Notes:

_____

_____

_____

_____

_____

Visited With: _____

Best Time of Year to Visit: _____Visit Again: Y / N

Perch Pub Brewery

232 S Wall St, Chandler, 85225
480-773-7688

Date Visited: _____

Rating: 🍺 🍺 🍺 🍺 🍺

stamp

BEERS TRIED:

_____

_____

_____

🍴 🚲 🏍️

ADDITIONAL SPECIAL FEATURES:

Happy Hour   Brunch
Outdoor Rooftop Seating   Bird Rescue

Favorite Brew – Likes – Dislikes – Notes:

_____

_____

_____

_____

_____

Visited With: _____

Best Time of Year to Visit: _____Visit Again: Y / N

Richter Aleworks

8279 W Lake Pleasant Pkwy, #109, Peoria, 85382
602-908-6553

Date Visited: _____

Rating: 🍺 🍺 🍺 🍺 🍺

stamp

BEERS TRIED:

_____

_____

_____

🎸 🚲 🏍 ⚙ 🚐

ADDITIONAL SPECIAL FEATURES:

Outside Food Allowed

Favorite Brew – Likes – Dislikes – Notes:

_____

_____

_____

_____

_____

Visited With: _____

Best Time of Year to Visit: _____ Visit Again: Y / N

Saddle Mountain Brewing Company

15651 W Roosevelt St, Goodyear, 85338
623-249-5520

Date Visited: _____

Rating: 🍺 🍺 🍺 🍺 🍺

stamp

BEERS TRIED:

_____

_____

_____

🍴 🐾 🚲 🏍️

ADDITIONAL SPECIAL FEATURES:

Happy Hour

Outdoor Seating   Kid Friendly

Favorite Brew – Likes – Dislikes – Notes:

_____

_____

_____

_____

_____

Visited With: _____

Best Time of Year to Visit: _____Visit Again: Y / N

SanTan Brewing Company –

Chandler Location
8 S San Marcos Pl, Chandler, 85225
480-917-8700

Date Visited: _____

Rating: 🍺 🍺 🍺 🍺 🍺   stamp

BEERS TRIED:

_____

_____

_____

🍴 🐾 🚲 🏍

ADDITIONAL SPECIAL FEATURES:

Happy Hour

Outdoor Seating   Kid Friendly

Favorite Brew – Likes – Dislikes – Notes:

_____

_____

_____

_____

_____

Visited With: _____

Best Time of Year to Visit: _____ Visit Again: Y / N

SanTan Brewing Company –

Phoenix Location

1525 E Bethany Home Rd, Phoenix, 85014
602-595-7390

Date Visited: _____

Rating: 🍺 🍺 🍺 🍺 🍺   stamp

BEERS TRIED:

_____

_____

_____

ADDITIONAL SPECIAL FEATURES:

Happy Hour
Kid Friendly

Favorite Brew – Likes – Dislikes – Notes:

_____

_____

_____

_____

_____

Visited With: _____

Best Time of Year to Visit: _____ Visit Again: Y / N

Scottsdale Beer Company

8608 E Shea Blvd, Scottsdale, 85260
480-219-1844

Date Visited: _____

Rating: 🍺 🍺 🍺 🍺 🍺

stamp

BEERS TRIED:

_____

_____

_____

🍴 🐾 🚲 🏍️

ADDITIONAL SPECIAL FEATURES:

Happy Hour

Outdoor Seating   Kid Friendly

Favorite Brew – Likes – Dislikes – Notes:

_____

_____

_____

_____

_____

Visited With: _____

Best Time of Year to Visit: _____Visit Again: Y / N

Sleepy Dog Saloon & Brewery

1920 E University Dr, #104, Tempe, 85281
480-967-5476

Date Visited: _____

Rating: 🍺 🍺 🍺 🍺 🍺

stamp

BEERS TRIED:

_____

_____

_____

🐾 🏍 ☸

ADDITIONAL SPECIAL FEATURES:

Happy Hour
Outside Food Allowed

Favorite Brew – Likes – Dislikes – Notes:

_____

_____

_____

_____

_____

Visited With: _____

Best Time of Year to Visit: _____Visit Again: Y / N

Sonoran Brewing Company

3002 E Washington St, Phoenix, 85034
602-510-8996

Date Visited: _____

Rating: 🍺 🍺 🍺 🍺 🍺   stamp

BEERS TRIED:

_____

_____

_____

🍴 🐾 🚲 🏍️

ADDITIONAL SPECIAL FEATURES:

Outside Food Allowed

Favorite Brew – Likes – Dislikes – Notes:

_____

_____

_____

_____

_____

Visited With: _____

Best Time of Year to Visit: _____Visit Again: Y / N

State 48 Funk House Brewery

6770 N Sunrise Blvd, G-100, Glendale, 85305
623-877-4448

Date Visited: _____

Rating: 🍺 🍺 🍺 🍺 🍺   stamp

BEERS TRIED:

_____

_____

_____

🍴 🐾 🚲 🏍 ❀

ADDITIONAL SPECIAL FEATURES:

Happy Hour
Bowling
Outdoor Seating   Kid Friendly

Favorite Brew – Likes – Dislikes – Notes:

_____

_____

_____

_____

_____

Visited With: _____

Best Time of Year to Visit: _____ Visit Again: Y / N

State 48 Brewery DTPHX

345 W Van Buren Street, Phoenix, AZ 85003

Date Visited: _____

Rating: 🍺 🍺 🍺 🍺 🍺

stamp

BEERS TRIED:

_____

_____

_____

ADDITIONAL SPECIAL FEATURES:

Happy Hour
Mezzanine
Outdoor Seating   Kid Friendly

Favorite Brew – Likes – Dislikes – Notes:

_____

_____

_____

_____

_____

Visited With: _____

Best Time of Year to Visit: _____Visit Again: Y / N

State 48 Brewery – Surprise

13823 W Bell Rd, Surprise, 85374
623-584-1095

Date Visited: _____

Rating: 🍺 🍺 🍺 🍺 🍺

stamp

BEERS TRIED:

_____

_____

_____

🍴 🐾 🚲 🏍 ☸

ADDITIONAL SPECIAL FEATURES:

Happy Hour

Outdoor Seating   Kid Friendly

Favorite Brew – Likes – Dislikes – Notes:

_____

_____

_____

_____

_____

Visited With: _____

Best Time of Year to Visit: _____Visit Again: Y / N

SunUp Brewing Company

322 E Camelback Rd, Phoenix, 85012
602-279-8909

Date Visited: _____

Rating: 🍺 🍺 🍺 🍺 🍺   stamp

BEERS TRIED:

_____

_____

_____

🍴 🐾 🚲

ADDITIONAL SPECIAL FEATURES:

Happy Hour
Shuffle Board
Outdoor Seating   Kid Friendly

Favorite Brew – Likes – Dislikes – Notes:

_____

_____

_____

_____

_____

Visited With: _____

Best Time of Year to Visit: _____Visit Again: Y / N

The Phoenix Ale Brewery

3002 E Washington St, Phoenix, 85034
602-275-5049

Date Visited: _____

Rating: 🍺 🍺 🍺 🍺 🍺

stamp

BEERS TRIED:

_____

_____

_____

🍴 🐾 🚲 🏍️

ADDITIONAL SPECIAL FEATURES:

Outside Food Allowed

Favorite Brew – Likes – Dislikes – Notes:

_____

_____

_____

_____

_____

Visited With: _____

Best Time of Year to Visit: _____Visit Again: Y / N

The Phoenix Ale Brewery Central Kitchen

5813 N 7th St, Phoenix, 85014
602-313-8713

Date Visited: _____

Rating: 🍺 🍺 🍺 🍺 🍺   stamp

BEERS TRIED:

_____

_____

_____

🍴 🐾 🚲 🏍 ⚙

ADDITIONAL SPECIAL FEATURES:

Outdoor Seating   Kid Friendly

Favorite Brew – Likes – Dislikes – Notes:

_____

_____

_____

_____

_____

Visited With: _____

Best Time of Year to Visit: _____ Visit Again: Y / N

The Shop Beer Co

922 W 1st St, Tempe, 85281
480-747-7316

Date Visited: _____

Rating: 🍺 🍺 🍺 🍺 🍺

stamp

BEERS TRIED:

_____

_____

_____

🚲 🏍 ✸

ADDITIONAL SPECIAL FEATURES:

Beer Garden

Favorite Brew – Likes – Dislikes – Notes:

_____

_____

_____

_____

_____

Visited With: _____

Best Time of Year to Visit: _____Visit Again: Y / N

Transplant City Beer Company

107 W Honeysuckle St, Litchfield Park, 85340

Date Visited: _____

Rating: 🍺 🍺 🍺 🍺 🍺

stamp

BEERS TRIED:

_____

_____

_____

🐾

ADDITIONAL SPECIAL FEATURES:

Kid Friendly

Favorite Brew – Likes – Dislikes – Notes:

_____

_____

_____

_____

_____

Visited With: _____

Best Time of Year to Visit: _____Visit Again: Y / N

Two Brothers Tap House and Brewery

4321 N Scottsdale Rd, Scottsdale, 85251
480-378-3001

Date Visited: _____

Rating: 🍺 🍺 🍺 🍺 🍺

stamp

BEERS TRIED:

_____

_____

_____

🍴 🐾 🚲

ADDITIONAL SPECIAL FEATURES:

Happy Hour
Outdoor Seating

Favorite Brew – Likes – Dislikes – Notes:

_____

_____

_____

_____

_____

Visited With: _____

Best Time of Year to Visit: _____Visit Again: Y / N

Uncle Bear's Brewery –

Phoenix Location

4921 E Ray Rd, #103, Phoenix, 85044

480-961-2374

Date Visited: _____

Rating: 🍺 🍺 🍺 🍺 🍺

stamp

BEERS TRIED:

_____

_____

_____

🍴 🐾 🚲 🏍️

ADDITIONAL SPECIAL FEATURES:

Happy Hour

Outdoor Seating   Kid Friendly

Favorite Brew – Likes – Dislikes – Notes:

_____

_____

_____

_____

_____

Visited With: _____

Best Time of Year to Visit: _____Visit Again: Y / N

Uncle Bear's Grill & Tap –

Mesa Location
9053 E Baseline Rd, #101A, Mesa, 85209
480-986-2228

Date Visited: _____

Rating: 🍺 🍺 🍺 🍺 🍺   stamp

BEERS TRIED:

_____

_____

_____

🍴 🐾 🚲 🏍

ADDITIONAL SPECIAL FEATURES:

Happy Hour

Outdoor Seating   Kid Friendly

Favorite Brew – Likes – Dislikes – Notes:

_____

_____

_____

_____

_____

Visited With: _____

Best Time of Year to Visit: _____Visit Again: Y / N

Uncle Bear's Grill & Tap –
Queen Creek Location
21151 E Rittenhouse Rd, Queen Creek, 85142
480-882-3177

Date Visited: _____

Rating: 🍺 🍺 🍺 🍺 🍺   stamp

BEERS TRIED:

_____

_____

_____

🍴 🐾 🚲 🏍️

ADDITIONAL SPECIAL FEATURES:

Happy Hour

Outdoor Seating   Kid Friendly

Favorite Brew – Likes – Dislikes – Notes:

_____

_____

_____

_____

_____

Visited With: _____

Best Time of Year to Visit: _____Visit Again: Y / N

Walter Station Brewery

4065 E Washington St, Phoenix, AZ 85034
602-368-8372

Date Visited: _____

Rating: 🍺 🍺 🍺 🍺 🍺

stamp

BEERS TRIED:

_____

_____

_____

🍴 🎸 🐾 🚲 🏍 ⚙

ADDITIONAL SPECIAL FEATURES:

Happy Hour

Outdoor Seating   Kid Friendly

Favorite Brew – Likes – Dislikes – Notes:

_____

_____

_____

_____

_____

Visited With: _____

Best Time of Year to Visit: _____Visit Again: Y / N

Wren House Brewing Company

2125 N 24th St, Phoenix, 85008
602-244-9184

Date Visited: _____

Rating: 🍺 🍺 🍺 🍺 🍺   stamp

BEERS TRIED:

_____

_____

_____

🐾 🚲 ☸

ADDITIONAL SPECIAL FEATURES:

Outside Food Allowed
Kid Friendly

Favorite Brew – Likes – Dislikes – Notes:

_____

_____

_____

_____

_____

Visited With: _____

Best Time of Year to Visit: _____Visit Again: Y / N

NORTHERN ARIZONA

ALPHABETICAL LISTING - Northern Arizona Breweries

Barley Brothers Brewery
Barnstar Brewing Company
Beaver Street Brewery
Black Bridge Brewery
Black Horse Brewery
College Street Brewery
Coppertop Alehouse
Dark Sky Brewing Co
Edge of the World Brewery
Flagstaff Brewing Company
Grand Canyon Brewing Company
Granite Mountain Brewing
Hangar 24 Brewery and Grill
Historic Brewing Barrel + Bottle House - Flagstaff
Historic Brewing Barrel + Bottle House - Williams
Historic Brewing Company
Insurgent Brewing
Lonesome Valley Brewing
Lumberyard Brewing Co
Mother Road Brewing Company - Butler
Mother Road Brewing Company - Southside
Mudshark Brewery and Public House
Oak Creek Brewery & Grill
Oak Creek Brewing Co
Pinetop Brewing Company
Prescott Brewing Company
RelicRoad Brewing Company
Rickety Cricket Brewing - Kingman
Rickety Cricket Brewing - Prescott
Sedona Beer Company
THAT Brewery - Cottonwood
THAT Brewery & Pub - Pine
Trail Crest Brewing Company
Verde Brewing Company
Wanderlust Brewing Company

Barley Brothers Brewery

1425 McCulloch Blvd, Lake Havasu City, 86403
928-505-7837

Date Visited: _____

Rating: 🍺 🍺 🍺 🍺 🍺

stamp

BEERS TRIED:

_____

_____

_____

🍴

ADDITIONAL SPECIAL FEATURES:

Happy Hour
Kid Friendly

Favorite Brew – Likes – Dislikes – Notes:

_____

_____

_____

_____

_____

Visited With: _____

Best Time of Year to Visit: _____Visit Again: Y / N

Barnstar Brewing Company

4050 N Forest Service 102 Rd, Skull Valley, 86338

928-442-2337

Date Visited: _____

Rating: 🍺 🍺 🍺 🍺 🍺   stamp

BEERS TRIED:

_____

_____

_____

🍴 🐾 ❀

ADDITIONAL SPECIAL FEATURES:

3 mile dirt road to location

Outdoor Seating   Kid Friendly

Outside Food Allowed

Favorite Brew – Likes – Dislikes – Notes:

_____

_____

_____

_____

_____

Visited With: _____

Best Time of Year to Visit: _____Visit Again: Y / N

Beaver Street Brewery

11 S Beaver St, #1, Flagstaff, 86001
928-779-0079

Date Visited: _____

Rating: 🍺 🍺 🍺 🍺 🍺

stamp

BEERS TRIED:

_____

_____

_____

🍴

ADDITIONAL SPECIAL FEATURES:

Happy Hour
Pool Tables
Outdoor Seating   Kid Friendly

Favorite Brew – Likes – Dislikes – Notes:

_____

_____

_____

_____

_____

Visited With: _____

Best Time of Year to Visit: _____Visit Again: Y / N

Black Bridge Brewery

421 E Beale St, Kingman, 86401
928-377-3618

Date Visited: _____

Rating: 🍺 🍺 🍺 🍺 🍺

BEERS TRIED:

_____

_____

_____

ADDITIONAL SPECIAL FEATURES:

Happy Hour
Outside Food Allowed
Outdoor Seating   Kid Friendly

Favorite Brew – Likes – Dislikes – Notes:

_____

_____

_____

_____

_____

Visited With: _____

Best Time of Year to Visit: _____Visit Again: Y / N

Black Horse Brewery

1058 Burton Rd, Show Low, 85901
928-537-9349

Date Visited: _____

Rating: 🍺 🍺 🍺 🍺 🍺

stamp

BEERS TRIED:

_____

_____

_____

ADDITIONAL SPECIAL FEATURES:

Outside Food Allowed

Outdoor Seating   Kid Friendly

Favorite Brew – Likes – Dislikes – Notes:

_____

_____

_____

_____

_____

Visited With: _____

Best Time of Year to Visit: _____Visit Again: Y / N

College Street Brewery

1940 College Drive, Lake Havasu City, 86403
928-854-2739

Date Visited: _____

Rating: 🍺 🍺 🍺 🍺 🍺   stamp

BEERS TRIED:

_____

_____

_____

🍴

ADDITIONAL SPECIAL FEATURES:

Happy Hour
Outdoor Patio

Favorite Brew – Likes – Dislikes – Notes:

_____

_____

_____

_____

_____

Visited With: _____

Best Time of Year to Visit: _____Visit Again: Y / N

Coppertop Alehouse

220 S Montezuma St, Prescott, 86303
928-351-7712

Date Visited: _____

Rating: 🍺 🍺 🍺 🍺 🍺

stamp

BEERS TRIED:

_____

_____

_____

ADDITIONAL SPECIAL FEATURES:

_____

Favorite Brew – Likes – Dislikes – Notes:

_____

_____

_____

_____

_____

Visited With: _____

Best Time of Year to Visit: _____ Visit Again: Y / N

Dark Sky Brewing Co

117 N Beaver St, A, Flagstaff, 86001
928-235-4525

Date Visited: _____

Rating: 🍺 🍺 🍺 🍺 🍺   stamp

BEERS TRIED:

_____

_____

_____

🐾 ☸ 🚐

ADDITIONAL SPECIAL FEATURES:

Happy Hour
Outdoor Seating

Favorite Brew – Likes – Dislikes – Notes:

_____

_____

_____

_____

_____

Visited With: _____

Best Time of Year to Visit: _____Visit Again: Y / N

Edge of The World Brewery

70 N Central St, Colorado City, 86021
928-875-8710

Date Visited: _____

Rating: 🍺 🍺 🍺 🍺 🍺

stamp

BEERS TRIED:

_____

_____

_____

🍴 🏍️ ☸️

ADDITIONAL SPECIAL FEATURES:

Kid Friendly

Favorite Brew – Likes – Dislikes – Notes:

_____

_____

_____

_____

_____

Visited With: _____

Best Time of Year to Visit: _____Visit Again: Y / N

Flagstaff Brewing Company

16 E Route 66, Flagstaff, 86001
928-773-1442

Date Visited: _____

Rating: 🍺 🍺 🍺 🍺 🍺   stamp

BEERS TRIED:

_____

_____

_____

🍴 🎸 🐾 🚲

ADDITIONAL SPECIAL FEATURES:

Outdoor Seating
Kid Friendly

Favorite Brew – Likes – Dislikes – Notes:

_____

_____

_____

_____

_____

Visited With: _____

Best Time of Year to Visit: _____Visit Again: Y / N

Grand Canyon Brewing Company

301 N 7th St, Williams, 86046
800-513-2072

Date Visited: _____

Rating: 🍺 🍺 🍺 🍺 🍺   stamp

BEERS TRIED:

_____

_____

_____

🍴 🎸 🏍 ⚙

ADDITIONAL SPECIAL FEATURES:

Happy Hour
Kid Friendly

Favorite Brew – Likes – Dislikes – Notes:

_____

_____

_____

_____

_____

Visited With: _____

Best Time of Year to Visit: _____Visit Again: Y / N

Granite Mountain Brewing

123 N Cortez St, Prescott, 86301
928-778-5535

Date Visited: _____

Rating: 🍺 🍺 🍺 🍺 🍺

stamp

BEERS TRIED:

_____

_____

_____

🎸 🐾 ✸

ADDITIONAL SPECIAL FEATURES:

Outdoor Seating
Outside Food Allowed

Favorite Brew – Likes – Dislikes – Notes:

_____

_____

_____

_____

_____

Visited With: _____

Best Time of Year to Visit: _____Visit Again: Y / N

Hangar 24 Brewery and Grill

5600 AZ-95, #6, Lake Havasu City, 86404
928-846-4447

Date Visited: _____

Rating: 🍺 🍺 🍺 🍺 🍺

stamp

BEERS TRIED:

_____

_____

_____

ADDITIONAL SPECIAL FEATURES:

Outdoor Seating
Kid Friendly

Favorite Brew – Likes – Dislikes – Notes:

_____

_____

_____

_____

_____

Visited With: _____

Best Time of Year to Visit: _____Visit Again: Y / N

Historic Brewing Barrel + Bottle House –

San Francisco Street Location

110 S San Francisco St, Flagstaff, 86001

928-774-0454

Date Visited: _____

Rating: 🍺 🍺 🍺 🍺 🍺   stamp

BEERS TRIED:

_____

_____

_____

🍴 🐾

ADDITIONAL SPECIAL FEATURES:

Happy Hour

Outdoor seating   Kid Friendly

Favorite Brew – Likes – Dislikes – Notes:

_____

_____

_____

_____

_____

Visited With: _____

Best Time of Year to Visit: _____Visit Again: Y / N

Historic Brewing Barrel + Bottle House

Williams Location

141 W Railroad Ave, Williams, 86046

928-635-5325

Date Visited: _____

Rating: 🍺 🍺 🍺 🍺 🍺   stamp

BEERS TRIED:

_____

_____

_____

🍴 🐾

ADDITIONAL SPECIAL FEATURES:

Happy Hour

Outdoor seating   Kid Friendly

Favorite Brew – Likes – Dislikes – Notes:

_____

_____

_____

_____

_____

Visited With: _____

Best Time of Year to Visit: _____Visit Again: Y / N

Historic Brewing Company –

Huntington Drive Location

4366 E Huntington Dr, Flagstaff, 86004

855-484-4677

Date Visited: _____

Rating: 🍺 🍺 🍺 🍺 🍺   stamp

BEERS TRIED:

_____

_____

_____

🐾 ☸ 🚐

ADDITIONAL SPECIAL FEATURES:

Outdoor Seating

Favorite Brew – Likes – Dislikes – Notes:

_____

_____

_____

_____

_____

Visited With: _____

Best Time of Year to Visit: _____Visit Again: Y / N

Insurgent Brewing

990 N Hwy 89, Suite B, Chino Valley, 86323
928-925-4773

Date Visited: _____

Rating: 🍺 🍺 🍺 🍺 🍺

BEERS TRIED:

_____

_____

_____

ADDITIONAL SPECIAL FEATURES:

_____

Favorite Brew – Likes – Dislikes – Notes:

_____

_____

_____

_____

_____

Visited With: _____

Best Time of Year to Visit: _____Visit Again: Y / N

Lonesome Valley Brewing

3040 N Windsong Dr, #101, Prescott Valley, 86314
928-515-3541

Date Visited: _____

Rating: 🍺 🍺 🍺 🍺 🍺   stamp

BEERS TRIED:

_____

_____

_____

🍴 🎸 ❀

ADDITIONAL SPECIAL FEATURES:

Outdoor Seating
Kid Friendly

Favorite Brew – Likes – Dislikes – Notes:

_____

_____

_____

_____

_____

Visited With: _____

Best Time of Year to Visit: _____Visit Again: Y / N

Lumberyard Brewing Co

5 S San Francisco St, Flagstaff, 86001
928-779-2739

Date Visited: _____

Rating: 🍺 🍺 🍺 🍺 🍺

stamp

BEERS TRIED:

_____

_____

_____

🍴

ADDITIONAL SPECIAL FEATURES:

Happy Hour
Outdoor Seating   Kid Friendly

Favorite Brew – Likes – Dislikes – Notes:

_____

_____

_____

_____

_____

Visited With: _____

Best Time of Year to Visit: _____Visit Again: Y / N

Mother Road Brewing Company – Butler Brewery

1300 Butler Ave, Suite 200, Flagstaff, 86001
928-774-0492

Date Visited: _____

Rating: 🍺 🍺 🍺 🍺 🍺   stamp

BEERS TRIED:

_____

_____

_____

🍴 🐾 🎯

ADDITIONAL SPECIAL FEATURES:

Happy Hour

Outdoor Seating   Kid Friendly

Favorite Brew – Likes – Dislikes – Notes:

_____

_____

_____

_____

_____

Visited With: _____

Best Time of Year to Visit: _____Visit Again: Y / N

Mother Road Brewing Company – Southside Brewery

7 S Mikes Pike St, Flagstaff, 86001
928-774-9139

Date Visited: _____

Rating: 🍺 🍺 🍺 🍺 🍺   stamp

BEERS TRIED:

_____

_____

_____

🍴 🐾 ✹

ADDITIONAL SPECIAL FEATURES:

Happy Hour
Outdoor Seating   Kid Friendly

Favorite Brew – Likes – Dislikes – Notes:

_____

_____

_____

_____

_____

Visited With: _____

Best Time of Year to Visit: _____Visit Again: Y / N

Mudshark Brewery and Public House

1095 Aviation Dr, Lake Havasu City, 86403
928-453-9302

Date Visited: _____

Rating: 🍺 🍺 🍺 🍺 🍺   stamp

BEERS TRIED:

_____

_____

_____

🍴 🎸 🐾 🚲 🏍 ☸

ADDITIONAL SPECIAL FEATURES:

Solar Powered Brewery

Outdoor Seating   Kid Friendly

Favorite Brew – Likes – Dislikes – Notes:

_____

_____

_____

_____

_____

Visited With: _____

Best Time of Year to Visit: _____ Visit Again: Y / N

Oak Creek Brewery & Grill

d201 336 AZ-179, Sedona, 86336
928-282-3300

Date Visited: _____

Rating: 🍺 🍺 🍺 🍺 🍺   stamp

BEERS TRIED:

_____

_____

_____

🍴

ADDITIONAL SPECIAL FEATURES:

Located in Tlaquepaque Arts & Shopping Village

Favorite Brew – Likes – Dislikes – Notes:

_____

_____

_____

_____

_____

Visited With: _____

Best Time of Year to Visit: _____Visit Again: Y / N

Oak Creek Brewing Co

2050 Yavapai Dr, #2C, Sedona, 86336
928-204-1300

Date Visited: _____

Rating: 🍺 🍺 🍺 🍺 🍺   stamp

BEERS TRIED:

_____

_____

_____

🍴 🍺

ADDITIONAL SPECIAL FEATURES:

Happy Hour

Outdoor Seating   Kid Friendly

Favorite Brew – Likes – Dislikes – Notes:

_____

_____

_____

_____

_____

Visited With: _____

Best Time of Year to Visit: _____Visit Again: Y / N

Pinetop Brewing Company

159 W White Mountain Blvd, Lakeside, 85929
928-358-1971

Date Visited: _____

Rating: 🍺 🍺 🍺 🍺 🍺

stamp

BEERS TRIED:

_____

_____

_____

🍴 🐾 🏍️

ADDITIONAL SPECIAL FEATURES:

Happy Hour
Dedicated Belgian Microbrewery
Kid Friendly   Outdoor Seating

Favorite Brew – Likes – Dislikes – Notes:

_____

_____

_____

_____

_____

Visited With: _____

Best Time of Year to Visit: _____Visit Again: Y / N

Prescott Brewing Company

130 W Gurley St, Prescott, 86301
928-771-2795

Date Visited: _____

Rating: 🍺 🍺 🍺 🍺 🍺   stamp

BEERS TRIED:

_____

_____

_____

🍴

ADDITIONAL SPECIAL FEATURES:

Kid Friendly

Favorite Brew – Likes – Dislikes – Notes:

_____

_____

_____

_____

_____

Visited With: _____

Best Time of Year to Visit: _____Visit Again: Y / N

RelicRoad Brewing Company

107 W 2nd St, Winslow, 86047
928-224-0045

Date Visited: _____

Rating: 🍺 🍺 🍺 🍺 🍺

stamp

BEERS TRIED:

_____

_____

_____

🍴 🐾 🎸 🏍

ADDITIONAL SPECIAL FEATURES:

Happy Hour

Outdoor Seating   Kid Friendly

Favorite Brew – Likes – Dislikes – Notes:

_____

_____

_____

_____

_____

Visited With: _____

Best Time of Year to Visit: _____ Visit Again: Y / N

Rickety Cricket Brewing

Kingman Location
312 E Beale St, Kingman, 86401
928-263-8444

Date Visited: _____

Rating: 🍺 🍺 🍺 🍺 🍺

stamp

BEERS TRIED:

_____

_____

_____

🍴 🐾 🚲 🏍 ☸

ADDITIONAL SPECIAL FEATURES:

Happy Hour

Outdoor Seating   Kid Friendly

Favorite Brew – Likes – Dislikes – Notes:

_____

_____

_____

_____

_____

Visited With: _____

Best Time of Year to Visit: _____ Visit Again: Y / N

Rickety Cricket Brewing

Prescott Location
214 S Montezuma St, Prescott, 86303
928-237-5510

Date Visited: _____

Rating: 🍺 🍺 🍺 🍺 🍺   stamp

BEERS TRIED:

_____

_____

_____

🍴 🎸 🐾 🚲 🏍 ⚙

ADDITIONAL SPECIAL FEATURES:

Happy Hour

Outdoor Seating   Kid Friendly

Favorite Brew – Likes – Dislikes – Notes:

_____

_____

_____

_____

_____

Visited With: _____

Best Time of Year to Visit: _____ Visit Again: Y / N

Sedona Beer Company

465 Jordan Rd, Sedona, 86336
928-862-4148

Date Visited: _____

Rating: 🍺 🍺 🍺 🍺 🍺   stamp

BEERS TRIED:

_____

_____

_____

🍴 🐾 🏍 ❀

ADDITIONAL SPECIAL FEATURES:

Outdoor Seating   Kid Friendly

Favorite Brew – Likes – Dislikes – Notes:

_____

_____

_____

_____

_____

Visited With: _____

Best Time of Year to Visit: _____ Visit Again: Y / N

THAT Brewery

Cottonwood Location
300 E Cherry St, Cottonwood, 86326
928-202-3013

Date Visited: _____

Rating: 🍺 🍺 🍺 🍺 🍺

stamp

BEERS TRIED:

_____

_____

_____

ADDITIONAL SPECIAL FEATURES:

Happy Hour   Kid Friendly
Outside Food Allowed

Favorite Brew – Likes – Dislikes – Notes:

_____

_____

_____

_____

_____

Visited With: _____

Best Time of Year to Visit: _____ Visit Again: Y / N

THAT Brewery & Pub

Pine Location

3270 N AZ Highway 87, Pine, 85544

928-476-3349

Date Visited: _____

Rating: 🍺 🍺 🍺 🍺 🍺   stamp

BEERS TRIED:

_____

_____

_____

🍴 👥 🎸 🏍 ⚙

ADDITIONAL SPECIAL FEATURES:

Happy Hour

Outdoor Seating   Kid Friendly

Favorite Brew – Likes – Dislikes – Notes:

_____

_____

_____

_____

_____

Visited With: _____

Best Time of Year to Visit: _____ Visit Again: Y / N

Trail Crest Brewing Company
1800 S Milton Rd, Suite 11, Flagstaff, 86001
928-440-5085

Date Visited: _____

Rating: 🍺 🍺 🍺 🍺 🍺   stamp

BEERS TRIED:

_____

_____

_____

🍴 🐾 🏍 ☸

ADDITIONAL SPECIAL FEATURES:

Happy Hour

Outdoor Seating   Kid Friendly

Favorite Brew – Likes – Dislikes – Notes:

_____

_____

_____

_____

_____

Visited With: _____

Best Time of Year to Visit: _____Visit Again: Y / N

Verde Brewing Company

724 Industrial Dr, #7a, Camp Verde, 86322
928-567-8626

Date Visited: _____

Rating: 🍺 🍺 🍺 🍺 🍺

stamp

BEERS TRIED:

_____

_____

_____

🍴 🎸 🐾 🏍 ⚙

ADDITIONAL SPECIAL FEATURES:

Happy Hour

Outdoor Seating   Kid Friendly

Favorite Brew – Likes – Dislikes – Notes:

_____

_____

_____

_____

_____

Visited With: _____

Best Time of Year to Visit: _____ Visit Again: Y / N

Wanderlust Brewing Company

1519 N Main St, #102, Flagstaff, 86004
928-351-7952

Date Visited: _____

Rating: 🍺 🍺 🍺 🍺 🍺

stamp

BEERS TRIED:

_____

_____

_____

ADDITIONAL SPECIAL FEATURES:

Outdoor Seating
Kid Friendly

Favorite Brew – Likes – Dislikes – Notes:

_____

_____

_____

_____

_____

Visited With: _____

Best Time of Year to Visit: _____Visit Again: Y / N

SOUTHERN ARIZONA

ALPHABETICAL LISTING - Southern Arizona Breweries

1912 Brewing Company
Barrio Brewing Co - Tucson
BlackRock Brewers
Borderlands Brewing Company
Button Brew House
Catalina Brewing Company
Copper Brothel Brewery
Copper Hop Ranch & Microbrewery
Copper Mine Brewing Co
Corbett Brewing Company
Crooked Tooth Brewing Co
Dillinger Brewing Company
Dragoon Brewing Company
Green Feet Brewing
Harbottle Brewing Company
Iron John's Brewing Company - Congress Ave
Iron John's Brewing Company - Plumer Ave
Old Bisbee Brewing Company
Prison Hill Brewing Company
Public Brewhouse
Pueblo Vida Brewing Company
Sentinel Peak Brewing Company
Ten 55 Brewing and Sausage House
The Address Brewing
Thunder Canyon Brewery Restaurant & Pub
Tombstone Brewing Company

1912 Brewing Company

2045 N Forbes Blvd, #105, Tucson, 85745
520-256-4851

Date Visited: _____

Rating: 🍺 🍺 🍺 🍺 🍺

stamp

BEERS TRIED:

_____

_____

_____

ADDITIONAL SPECIAL FEATURES:

Happy Hour

Favorite Brew – Likes – Dislikes – Notes:

_____

_____

_____

_____

_____

Visited With: _____

Best Time of Year to Visit: _____Visit Again: Y / N

Barrio Brewing Co –

Tucson Location
800 E 16th St, Tucson, 85719
520-791-2739

Date Visited: _____

Rating: 🍺 🍺 🍺 🍺 🍺

stamp

BEERS TRIED:

_____

_____

_____

ADDITIONAL SPECIAL FEATURES:

Happy Hour

Outdoor Seating   Kid Friendly

Favorite Brew – Likes – Dislikes – Notes:

_____

_____

_____

_____

_____

Visited With: _____

Best Time of Year to Visit: _____Visit Again: Y / N

BlackRock Brewers

1664 S Research Loop, #200, Tucson, 85710
520-207-3203

Date Visited: _____

Rating: 🍺 🍺 🍺 🍺 🍺   stamp

BEERS TRIED:

_____

_____

_____

ADDITIONAL SPECIAL FEATURES:

Pinball Machines
Kid Friendly

Favorite Brew – Likes – Dislikes – Notes:

_____

_____

_____

_____

_____

Visited With: _____

Best Time of Year to Visit: _____Visit Again: Y / N

Borderlands Brewing Company

119 E Toole Ave, Tucson, 85701
520-261-8773

Date Visited: _____

Rating: 🍺 🍺 🍺 🍺 🍺   stamp

BEERS TRIED:

_____

_____

_____

ADDITIONAL SPECIAL FEATURES:

Outdoor Seating
Kid Friendly

Favorite Brew – Likes – Dislikes – Notes:

_____

_____

_____

_____

_____

Visited With: _____

Best Time of Year to Visit: _____Visit Again: Y / N

Button Brew House

6800 N Camino Martin, Suite 160, Tucson, 85741
520-268-8543

Date Visited: _____

Rating: 🍺 🍺 🍺 🍺 🍺

stamp

BEERS TRIED:

_____

_____

_____

ADDITIONAL SPECIAL FEATURES:

Near Tucson Bike Loop
Outdoor Seating   Kid Friendly
Outside Food Allowed

Favorite Brew – Likes – Dislikes – Notes:

_____

_____

_____

_____

_____

Visited With: _____

Best Time of Year to Visit: _____Visit Again: Y / N

Catalina Brewing Company

6918 N Camino Martin, Suite 120, Tucson, 85741
520-329-3622

Date Visited: _____

Rating: 🍺 🍺 🍺 🍺 🍺

stamp

BEERS TRIED:

_____

_____

_____

🚲 🏍 ⚙ 🚐

ADDITIONAL SPECIAL FEATURES:

Happy Hour
Near Tucson Bike Loop
Outside Food Allowed

Favorite Brew – Likes – Dislikes – Notes:

_____

_____

_____

_____

_____

Visited With: _____

Best Time of Year to Visit: _____Visit Again: Y / N

Copper Brothel Brewery

3112 Highway 83, Sonoita, 85637
520-405-6721

Date Visited: _____

Rating: 🍺 🍺 🍺 🍺 🍺

stamp

BEERS TRIED:

_____

_____

_____

🍴 🎸 🏍 ⚙

ADDITIONAL SPECIAL FEATURES:

Happy Hour

Outdoor Seating   Kid Friendly

Favorite Brew – Likes – Dislikes – Notes:

_____

_____

_____

_____

_____

Visited With: _____

Best Time of Year to Visit: _____ Visit Again: Y / N

Copper Hop Ranch & Microbrewery

5 Fairview Ln, Elgin, 85611
520-455-4673

Date Visited: _____

Rating: 🍺 🍺 🍺 🍺 🍺

stamp

BEERS TRIED:

_____

_____

_____

🎸 🐾 🏍 ⚙

ADDITIONAL SPECIAL FEATURES:

Outdoor Seating
Kid Friendly

Favorite Brew – Likes – Dislikes – Notes:

_____

_____

_____

_____

_____

Visited With: _____

Best Time of Year to Visit: _____Visit Again: Y / N

Copper Mine Brewing Co

3455 S Palo Verde Rd, Tucson, 85713
520-333-6140

Date Visited: _____

Rating: 🍺 🍺 🍺 🍺 🍺   stamp

BEERS TRIED:

_____

_____

_____

🚲 🏍 ⚙ 🚐

ADDITIONAL SPECIAL FEATURES:

_____

Favorite Brew – Likes – Dislikes – Notes:

_____

_____

_____

_____

_____

Visited With: _____

Best Time of Year to Visit: _____Visit Again: Y / N

Corbett Brewing Company

417 N Herbert, Tucson, 85087
520-770-1600

Date Visited: _____

Rating: 🍺 🍺 🍺 🍺 🍺

stamp

BEERS TRIED:

_____

_____

_____

🎸 ⊛

ADDITIONAL SPECIAL FEATURES:

Outdoor Seating

Favorite Brew – Likes – Dislikes – Notes:

_____

_____

_____

_____

_____

Visited With: _____

Best Time of Year to Visit: _____Visit Again: Y / N

Crooked Tooth Brewing Co

228 E 6th St, Tucson, 85705
520-444-5305

Date Visited: _____

Rating: 🍺 🍺 🍺 🍺 🍺

stamp

BEERS TRIED:

_____

_____

_____

ADDITIONAL SPECIAL FEATURES:

Outside Food Allowed

Outdoor Seating   Kid Friendly

Favorite Brew – Likes – Dislikes – Notes:

_____

_____

_____

_____

_____

Visited With: _____

Best Time of Year to Visit: _____Visit Again: Y / N

Dillinger Brewing Company

3895 N Oracle Rd, Tucson, 85705
520-207-2312

Date Visited: _____

Rating: 🍺 🍺 🍺 🍺 🍺   stamp

BEERS TRIED:

_____

_____

_____

🎸 🐾 🎯 🚐

ADDITIONAL SPECIAL FEATURES:

Outside Food Allowed
Outdoor Seating   Kid Friendly

Favorite Brew – Likes – Dislikes – Notes:

_____

_____

_____

_____

_____

Visited With: _____

Best Time of Year to Visit: _____Visit Again: Y / N

Dragoon Brewing Company

1859 W Grant Rd, #111, Tucson, 85745
520-329-3606

Date Visited: _____

Rating: 🍺 🍺 🍺 🍺 🍺   stamp

BEERS TRIED:

_____

_____

_____

ADDITIONAL SPECIAL FEATURES:

Happy Hour
Outside Food Allowed

Favorite Brew – Likes – Dislikes – Notes:

_____

_____

_____

_____

_____

Visited With: _____

Best Time of Year to Visit: _____Visit Again: Y / N

Green Feet Brewing

3669 E 44th St, Tucson, 85713
520-977-1691

Date Visited: _____

Rating: 🍺 🍺 🍺 🍺 🍺

stamp

BEERS TRIED:

_____

_____

_____

ADDITIONAL SPECIAL FEATURES:

Happy Hour
Military Friendly

Favorite Brew – Likes – Dislikes – Notes:

_____

_____

_____

_____

_____

Visited With: _____

Best Time of Year to Visit: _____Visit Again: Y / N

Harbottle Brewing Company

3820 S Palo Verde Rd, #102, Tucson, 85714
520-305-9863

Date Visited: _____

Rating: 🍺 🍺 🍺 🍺 🍺   stamp

BEERS TRIED:

_____

_____

_____

ADDITIONAL SPECIAL FEATURES:

Outside Food Allowed

Favorite Brew – Likes – Dislikes – Notes:

_____

_____

_____

_____

_____

Visited With: _____

Best Time of Year to Visit: _____Visit Again: Y / N

Iron John's Brewing Company –

Congress Avenue Location
222 E Congress Ave, Tucson, 85701
520-232-2530

Date Visited: _____

Rating: 🍺 🍺 🍺 🍺 🍺   stamp

BEERS TRIED:

_____

_____

_____

🐾 ☸

ADDITIONAL SPECIAL FEATURES:

Happy Hour
Outside Food Allowed

Favorite Brew – Likes – Dislikes – Notes:

_____

_____

_____

_____

_____

Visited With: _____

Best Time of Year to Visit: _____Visit Again: Y / N

Iron John's Brewing Company –

Plumber Avenue Location

245 S Plumer Ave, #27, Tucson, 85719
520-775-1727

Date Visited: _____

Rating: 🍺 🍺 🍺 🍺 🍺

BEERS TRIED:

_____

_____

_____

ADDITIONAL SPECIAL FEATURES:

Happy Hour
Outside Food Allowed

Favorite Brew – Likes – Dislikes – Notes:

_____

_____

_____

_____

_____

Visited With: _____

Best Time of Year to Visit: _____Visit Again: Y / N

Old Bisbee Brewing Company

200 Brewery Ave, Bisbee, 85603
520-432-2739

Date Visited: _____

Rating: 🍺 🍺 🍺 🍺 🍺

stamp

BEERS TRIED:

_____

_____

_____

🍴 🐾 🏍 ⚙

ADDITIONAL SPECIAL FEATURES:

Outside Food Allowed

Outdoor Seating   Kid Friendly

Favorite Brew – Likes – Dislikes – Notes:

_____

_____

_____

_____

_____

Visited With: _____

Best Time of Year to Visit: _____Visit Again: Y / N

Prison Hill Brewing Company

278 S Main St, Yuma, 85364
928-276-4001

Date Visited: _____

Rating: 🍺 🍺 🍺 🍺 🍺

stamp

BEERS TRIED:

_____

_____

_____

🍴 🐾 🚲 🏍 ⚙

ADDITIONAL SPECIAL FEATURES:

Outdoor Seating
Kid Friendly

Favorite Brew – Likes – Dislikes – Notes:

_____

_____

_____

_____

_____

Visited With: _____

Best Time of Year to Visit: _____Visit Again: Y / N

Public Brewhouse

209 N Hoff Ave, Tucson, 85705
520-775-2337

Date Visited: _____

Rating: 🍺 🍺 🍺 🍺 🍺

BEERS TRIED:

_____

_____

_____

ADDITIONAL SPECIAL FEATURES:

Happy Hour
Outside Food Allowed

Favorite Brew – Likes – Dislikes – Notes:

_____

_____

_____

_____

_____

Visited With: _____

Best Time of Year to Visit: _____Visit Again: Y / N

Pueblo Vida Brewing Company

115 E Broadway Blvd, Tucson, 85701
520-623-7168

Date Visited: _____

Rating: 🍺 🍺 🍺 🍺 🍺

stamp

BEERS TRIED:

_____

_____

_____

ADDITIONAL SPECIAL FEATURES:

Outside Food Allowed

Favorite Brew – Likes – Dislikes – Notes:

_____

_____

_____

_____

_____

Visited With: _____

Best Time of Year to Visit: _____Visit Again: Y / N

Sentinel Peak Brewing Company

4746 E Grant Rd, Tucson, 85712
520-777-9456

Date Visited: _____

Rating: 🍺 🍺 🍺 🍺 🍺   stamp

BEERS TRIED:

_____

_____

_____

🍴 🐾 🚲 🏍 ☸

ADDITIONAL SPECIAL FEATURES:

Happy Hour

Outdoor Seating   Kid Friendly

Favorite Brew – Likes – Dislikes – Notes:

_____

_____

_____

_____

_____

Visited With: _____

Best Time of Year to Visit: _____Visit Again: Y / N

Ten 55 Brewing and Sausage House

110 E Congress St, Tucson, 85701
520-461-8073

Date Visited: _____

Rating: 🍺 🍺 🍺 🍺 🍺   stamp

BEERS TRIED:

_____

_____

_____

🍴 🎸 ☸

ADDITIONAL SPECIAL FEATURES:

German-Style Beer House

Favorite Brew – Likes – Dislikes – Notes:

_____

_____

_____

_____

_____

Visited With: _____

Best Time of Year to Visit: _____Visit Again: Y / N

The Address Brewing

1702 E Speedway Blvd, Tucson, 85719
520-325-1706

Date Visited: _____

Rating: 🍺 🍺 🍺 🍺 🍺

stamp

BEERS TRIED:

_____

_____

_____

🍴 ⚙

ADDITIONAL SPECIAL FEATURES:

Happy Hour
Kid Friendly

Favorite Brew – Likes – Dislikes – Notes:

_____

_____

_____

_____

_____

Visited With: _____

Best Time of Year to Visit: _____ Visit Again: Y / N

Thunder Canyon Brewery
Restaurant & Pub

220 E Broadway Blvd, Tucson, 85701
520-396-3480

Date Visited: _____

Rating: 🍺 🍺 🍺 🍺 🍺   stamp

BEERS TRIED:

_____

_____

_____

🍴 🐾 ☸

ADDITIONAL SPECIAL FEATURES:

Happy Hour
Distillery
Pool Tables   Kid Friendly

Favorite Brew – Likes – Dislikes – Notes:

_____

_____

_____

_____

_____

Visited With: _____

Best Time of Year to Visit: _____Visit Again: Y / N

Tombstone Brewing Company

107 E Toughnut St, Tombstone, 85638
520-222-6781

Date Visited: _____

Rating: 🍺 🍺 🍺 🍺 🍺   stamp

BEERS TRIED:

_____

_____

_____

ADDITIONAL SPECIAL FEATURES:

Outdoor Seating

Favorite Brew – Likes – Dislikes – Notes:

_____

_____

_____

_____

_____

Visited With: _____

Best Time of Year to Visit: _____Visit Again: Y / N

ADDITIONAL NOTES

_____

_____

_____

_____

_____

_____

_____

_____

_____

_____

_____

_____

_____

_____

_____

_____

_____

_____

_____

_____

_____

_____

Made in the USA
Columbia, SC
20 October 2018